Luck in Haphazard Calligraphy

Poems by Mark Putzi

Compiled with Introduction and Commentary by Scott J. Shappell, M.D., Ph.D.

"A Painting" was previously published in Darkling Magazine in 2006; "Building" was previously published in Karamu, Volume XX, No 2, Spring 2007; "The Jugglers" was previously published in Fox Cry Review, Volume XXXII, September 2006; "Tattoo" was previously published in Heartlands, Volume 4, Fall 2006.

Introduction copyright 2012 by Scott B. Shappell.

Hekaśa Books are available at quantity discounts with bulk purchase for educational, business, or sales promotional use.

For information, please contact:
Hekaśa Publishing
1920 Abrams Parkway, #400
Dallas, TX 75214-6218
Phone: 214-321-4158
Fax: 214-827-5292
Email: info@hekasa.com
www.hekasa.com

Book Design by Scott Baber
Cover Graphic by Travis Scott Lee Shappell

ISBN: (13 digit) 978-0-9832293-1-5

Table of Contents

Introduction

The first time I met Mark Putzi was in January 2011. His brother, Matt Putzi, and I have been close friends for several years. Large to the same intimidating degree as Matt (about 6'3" and over 300 lbs.) and compounded with the unavoidable (even to the most liberal of minds) lurking concerns regarding his history of a serious psychological diagnosis, there could be no argument to my noting that if Mark wanted to break me into pieces...he could easily break me into pieces. However, Mark's resemblance to Matt made me feel an instant kinship with him.

At that time, Mark said something in passing that intrigued me; basically that all writers have (or if dead, have had) a big ego (i.e., a strong sense of self), except for maybe Mayakovsky. Such a statement, coming from such a source, seemed important to me literary wise, and it especially loomed in my mind as possibly holding a clue to Mark as a poet as well. In my recent re-connection to poetry following being diagnosed with ALS in April of 2009, I had read some Russian poets of the peri-Revolution periods, including Akhmatova and Mandelstam[1]. In subsequent consideration of the life and poetry of the briefly Futurist, pro-Bolshevik, and Soviet propagandist Mayakovsky, his larger than life persona and the manifestations of his megalomaniac manner (including in his verse)[2] painted Mark's comment either as unexpected concrete sarcasm or as piercing psychological and literary insight. It can be appreciated that underneath Mayakovsky's bravado and bold phrasings there was a surprising selflessness and a willingness to serve. He was committed to a cause for the Russian people (in the Bolshevik revolution and solidification of a communist Soviet state) in which his role within the social, literary, and political circumstances may have required such a personality and writing style as some sort of psychological counter-balance. Regardless of whether he may have been predisposed to such, he thrust that entire ego behind that cause in a fashion incapable of compromise, eventuating one of the greatest sums ever extracted from an artist.

Despite the differences in times and sociopolitical backgrounds, it is this willingness to not ignore but to bear the full brunt of the burden placed upon an individual by one's non-ideal and staggeringly demanding surroundings that I find similar in Mark Putzi's poetry to that of the legendary Russian Mayakovsky. Here we find some of the extremes of art expressed from the deepest places of the human psyche. Readers of this type of poetry benefit from these artists on whom have been exacted the very large price of coping, reflecting, and expressing. As Mayakovsky wrote in the 1926 poem "Conversation With a Tax Collector About Poetry":

Look here-
            how much I've lost,
what
        expenses
            I have in my production
and how much I spend
                on materials.[3]

There are many different types of man-made hell on earth. Some are epic, like the Bolshevik Revolution occurring within a Russia already strained by the First World War, and giving rise to a long period of oppression within the not so ideal Communism of the Stalin-tainted Soviet state. Some are far more subtle, affecting smaller numbers of individuals in scenarios that won't topple empires or provide a basis for grand movies. What does all this have to do with poetry? Much . . . and specifically to the poetry written by Mark Putzi. Mark's poetry illustrates the full spectrum of human nature; from the circumstances underlying its origins to the spirit that allows a voice to rise above the blackness of selfishness and evil that permeates our planet like a poisonous ether rising from the pathetic container of non-enlightenment. We must be aware that the same insecurities and social malad-justments that lead to wars, holocausts, and genocides are evident within hideous interpersonal acts on a daily basis. Destroying a whole lot of people in a whole lot of acts one at a time is not that fundamentally different. Mark Putzi's poetry is a tornado through the still breeze we artificially perfume ourselves in.

Most of what I know about Mark's background and family I have learned from his brother Matt, who is one year younger than Mark. Matt is a pathologist with special focus in prostate pathology (my main area of clinical and research work in the last twelve or so years as a physician-scientist). I'd certainly gathered that there were some "problems" within Matt's and Mark's family. I learned more details as I became specifically interested in how his experiences and family relationships may have contributed to Mark's poetry. Some of these are shared here in the interest of poetry, as inherent dispositions mixed with needs arising from human interactions shape personalities and psyches reflected, however directly or indirectly, in art of a potentially truly transcendent nature[5]. It appears to me that the less than ideal up-bringing of the brothers Putzi is a factor in Mark's past struggles with mental health and the beautifully sensitive poetry that has emerged from this extra challenge.

As I try to fathom anyone surviving even mildly emotionally- or psychologi-cally- intact in the environment in which Matt and Mark were raised, it's easy to understand why these brothers, extraordinarily intelligent and preciously sensitive, still deal daily with the psychopathological anvils that were stacked upon their young shoulders. In addition to the usual demands of school, the brothers were basically forced at an early age to work for their father's various construction endeavors in a fashion and to a degree that is very socially abnormal. Their father would commonly not even go to work, but still find time to spy on the kids to make sure that THEY (students in junior high and high school) were working. There were abundant episodes of real and extreme danger. In one, 16 year old Matt was guiding a cement shoot in a tight space and was caught under a collapsed wall. This was witnessed by 17 year-old Mark, in attendance during the hour-long rescue excavation. Mark, naturally upset, reported the incident to their mother. Yet later, briefed by her husband, their father, she stood the "company line" and said that the incident never happened! This is but one indication of a domestic environment that to those of us raised in fairly normal loving families sounds bizarre to the point of unreality. Of note, and a likely contributing factor, Mark's father was an alcoholic. (Mark is a recovering alcoholic.)

There is substantial reason to regard abnormal childhood environments as being major contributing factors to schizophrenia and related disorders (e.g., as reflected in existence of terms such as "schizophrenogenic mother"). In Mark and Matt's childhood home in Milwaukee, Wisconsin, their father, John, would go months without talking to his children; commonly just staring at them, unblinkingly, for twenty to thirty minutes at a time. This was a group of siblings of uniformly high intelligence and strong academic aptitude, yet all five children would eventually require at least therapy at some point. Margaret ("Margie"), the oldest, has a Ph.D. in Education. Next to youngest Marie, an amateur botanist, was previously a water chemistry scientist, giving it up for a Master's Degree in Writing, and now having returned to school for a Masters or Ph.D. in Psychology. Matt, the second oldest boy, completed a double undergraduate major in Philosophy and Zoology at the University of Wisconsin, Milwaukee. Attending college locally was a prerequisite for Mark and Matt to live at home, by which they could not only save money, but especially contribute to family finances by continuing to work construction. Matt eventually left, first attending Graduate School in Anthropology at the University of California at Davis and then Medical School at Tufts University in Boston. Matt completed the five year residency training in Anatomic and Clinical Pathology at the University of Michigan Medical Center and began further training at Johns Hopkins, an opportunity basically obliterated when he "bottomed out" during a painful divorce. Matt would eventually recover to become a highly functioning part of a series of reference laboratories where he performs diagnostic services as a very strong genitourinary pathologist. As rocky a road as this was, older brother Mark fared less well.

Mark not only stayed at home and worked construction related to his father's typically ill-fated endeavors while in college, but that's exactly what his life was after college. Mark also studied at the University of Wisconsin, Milwaukee, beginning in Psychology, then graduating with a degree in Creative Writing. After graduating, he continued to live at home and work for his father. Well versed and muscled in construction labor by now, Mark ran a construction crew, but was paid basically like a "grunt laborer", not discernibly different than when he started at age 13. The pathos of that unhealthy environment was apparently covered up collectively, with Mark's unique intelligence and abilities buried within the same shovelings. It is hard for me to truly imagine the day-in and day-out wear and the stretched to the limits coping mechanisms required during this more than a decade long period in which, really, Mark should have been variously participating in some of the usual post-college life tasks and encountering and learning from the (normal) little ups and downs in the steady course of gaining progressive self-responsibility. In fact, the lack of a reasonable dose of these usual "real-world" encounters surfaces in some of the investigations related in Mark's poems. It is a tribute to the magnitude of inherent absorption of an unquenched thirst of a richly thinking and feeling insight and the pure striving of psyche that we are gifted in Mark's verse with a consequently fresh look at things that we have collectively staled in our society over time.

Mark was still working for his strange father (though no longer living at home) when he was first diagnosed as schizophrenic at the age of 33 in 1994. Mark quit drinking in 1995. He started writing poetry around the year 2000, corresponding to what he notes as the acquisition of a hard earned greater spiritual maturity. Most of the poems contained within this collection were written between 2001 and 2007. The severity of the challenges he has faced can readily be imagined through the content of many of the poems. Poetry prompted by and reflecting the abnormal psychological conditions Mark was contained within may have represented an important compensatory mechanism, a necessary channeling of emotions while grasping for psychological and spiritual healing. Facilitated by a powerful brain and a natural creative ability, the possible progress of this heroic effort forms the mental image with which I have chosen the order for the poems, allowing, of course, for certain overlapping themes. However, each poem clearly stands on its own, and they can be read in any order. Titles for those poems within these loose groups are listed at the beginning of the Introduction sections in which they are discussed. I hope that some readers may find this ordering useful towards appreciating another dimension of Mark's powerful poetry, an honest presentation of an incredible, and on-going, journey. As I read the poems, then, I came up with topics like: *Childhood Innocence and Issues of Perspective* (Poems 1,2); *Fucked Up People and the Damage That They Do* (Poems 3,4,5); *The Bland Medical Approach to Psychological Healing and Reduced Experience of Life by its Objectivizing* (Poems 6,7,8); *The Long-Term Consequences Regarding Romance* (Poems 9,10,11); *The Scarred Poet's Insight into Life* (Poems 12,13,14,15,16)…*And Into Scarring* (Poems 17,18); *A Brilliant Perspective* (or, *Seeing Things With the Refreshing Poet's Mind*) (Poems 19,20,21,22); *An Earned Right to Analyze* (or, *The Light in the Surviving Forest*) (Poems 23,24); and *Rebirth* (Poems 25,26). As some readers may prefer to consider any commentary regarding specific poems in smaller aliquots to match the prior or subsequent reading of the actual poems, the remainder of the Introduction has the poem titles from such groupings listed at the start of the comments related to them.

My Uncle's Mexico, Elegy

This first poem is a wonderful exploration of the underappreciated theme of child versus adult perspective. The exotic background serves very well as a launching point for the psychological considerations. In places like Tijuana, which thrive because of the very people like the poem's uncle, the youth perceived bizarre and mysterious nature of "sombreros, stick puppets" and orgy of bright colors do indeed reside in a "pile of rubbish" (as perceived by the older human). Not to detract from all the wonderful features of Mexico and Mexican heritage, but the best features are not necessarily displayed in border towns with their particular flavors of vices and cheap souvenirs. The word "indicate" is a well-chosen one for the way in which a child is looking to receive what he sees through car windows and store windows as presented by his theoretically responsible adult, the tour guide, like a fairy or good witch in a children's story.

Within the mystery of this colorful foreign world come also the child-interpreted implications of the various sordid acts (likely "indicated" by the Uncle who may be winking or have his fingers crossed behind his back). It is the eyes of children who see "kin" instead of hidden girlfriends (or brief recreational travel companions). This perspective is no longer available to the adult, which begs the question: Why? (after all, they used to have it). Perhaps it was lost long ago during all the years of THIS:

..........................Al, you impressed your ten-year old nephew
With otherworldly knowledge, with stories of a nation-wide
Siesta. You stopped in Texas long enough to drop off
Your dark girlfriend at her cousin's. ....

Elegy is another provocative exploration of perspective; one that may not sit all that well with those who are comfortable within collective ego-protected narrow national identities. It seems pretty clear that this poem was written following "9-11", the date (9/11/2001) that two jet planes were flown into the World Trade Center Towers in New York. The first stanza is an insightful, maybe only partially metaphorical statement on the nature of human memory:

Everyone who saw this
Wrote a poem in their heads
As soon as it happened.
It's the way we remember.

Most everyone likely appreciates that emotion and setting can be powerful stimuli to provoke the recall of a certain memory. However, context and emotion are themselves crucial components of what and how we remember[6]. Maybe unlike the silicone chips we sometimes try to compare with ourselves, our memories are not stored static pieces of visual, auditory, or other sensory input bits, later "pulled-up" in flawlessly faithful form. We construct with emotion, emotion based on strongly reinforced opinions, all part of the ego-scaffolding; that is, we "write poems".

The dark sadness and shock that this event (and others like it) presents to us are further ensured by the media showing it "again and again / For many days thereafter". The media is, of course, an important guardian and supplier of some of the shared tools by which we construct not only our responses, but our reinforced prejudices, as conveyed in the particularly powerful metaphor of "multiple surgeries...":

And then to see it again and again
For many days thereafter:
It was like multiple surgeries
Of the same resected bowel.

In the midst of the expressions of reactionary rage and self-preservation modes, the poet himself "described not feeling". Perhaps this is the "response" from the inevitable eventual state of the overly-sensitive poet exposed over and over and over again to the cruel acts of human beings. Sometimes then, the poet brave enough to see more universally can seem so different from everyone else - the loud, unruly, and potentially volatile mob with their "us" versus "them" mentality.

Instead, the poet wonders about the thousands of simultaneously killed victims:

And I wondered what cry
Did their souls send up
Into the imperious heavens…?

The reference in the next stanza to the "Everlasting Om?" is an indictment of all of those who praise the name of God and act not according to true God-realization[7]. Perhaps no civilization in the history of the world is quite as adept as the United States at presenting itself as the power of good fighting the evil forces of darkness, the "American Zeus". The poem concludes:

…Now we know

What it was like for Japan in '45
Hit not once but twice.

Now before some nationalistically, religiously defined member of the "us" in this circumstance takes offence at comparing "our" experienced tragedy to that of any other event, that's neither the intent nor the point here. These are all tragic, as were the surprise attack on Pearl Harbor and the fire-bombings of Dresden and Tokyo, killing more than a hundred thousand civilians. Oh sad indeed that this list could be so much longer. It is fallacy to suggest that one hideous act of humans is more tragic than another; but it's also fallacy to keep perpetuating the circumstances in which one must argue which heinous acts are more "justified". All these mass slaughtered people are simply those trying to go about their day in a world where just the "regular" things seem hard enough, as the poet conveys from a woman witnessing the latest disaster from the perspective of being seven months pregnant: "All I give a fuck about is this baby."

7

This poem does NOT detract from the victims of "9-11". If anything, it begs, as so many non-answered wishes like it before, towards an objective that is so unlikely it has become repressed into the form of cliché: "that their death not be in vain." The poet provides the much needed perspective of a broader humanity.

*   *   *

Addict, Lumberjack and Wife, To a Seamstress

Towards the more personal sides of experience now, *Addict* is an eerie poem. It begins,

> *The quiet man descends, having awakened*
> *In himself a certain intellectual curiosity.*

We know a quiet man, one with large intellectual capacity. As related to the poem's narrative, it would be easy to forgive such a man for taking a sword or any other weapon and then sneaking up (moving by "whispers with his feet") and maybe fixing a thing or two. Indeed, if the conditions were examined intellectually, objectively, outside of possibly handicapping psychological factors, such action may make the most sense. Though we're used to thinking of a "leap of faith" as an act after reasoning capabilities have been exceeded and of rational acts as being steady and stepwise, here it is instead the killer's brain and his intelligence that have allowed him to finally make that precious breakthrough to a level of potentially "addicting" bliss.

> *The one left standing contemplates the meandering*
> *Circus of his fears, and with a rational leap*
> *Expounds upon the rightness of his kill.*

Perhaps we are witnessing an apparently justifiable homicide, when the seemingly mad one finally screams to himself, "stop the (real) madness!" Then, in an interesting twist on a Nietzsche maxim, "Whatever doesn't kill me can only hospitalize me," the freakishly intelligent new killer considers likely long pondered facts from the specific guidebooks of the law-abiding society in which such hideous (real) crimes have been perpetrated against him. The poem concludes with two lines of macabre imagery in which we see how hard it must be to not want to seek again such an ecstatic feeling of liberation.

Lumberjack and Wife is a staggeringly good, albeit disturbing poem. I find the two line stanza form to be particularly effective. It immediately reminded me of Sylvia Plath's poem "The Thin People", which also uses two line stanzas. This is perhaps my favorite poem of Plath's *Colossus*, probably because of the shear ache it puts diffusely into and around me. In her poem, the two-line stanzas serve to reinforce the notion of thinness:

It was only in a movie, it was only
In a war making evil headlines when we

Were small that they famished and
Grew so lean and would not round

Out their stalky limbs again though peace
Plumped the bellies of the mice[8]

Mark's *Lumberjack and Wife* stanza form gives it a rigid or regular structure, much like the work and end-products of a lumberjack, the "geometry" whereby the devastating consequences of the presented relationship should be knowable. "Everything must be reduced to its elemental state" seems to reflect the black and white in which so many try to see and hopelessly understand things, the x and y axes of the "moaning" gray of our daily lives and complex relationships as elaborated in the next stanza:

Between the vertical and the horizontal is a crashing arc of moaning limbs.
I with my saw carefully place its descent.

One can't help but suspect personal references (regardless of how literal or not) in detailed lines such as:

At home her lover muses and she smokes and feigns indifference.

Feigning indifference is one of the many ways in which we protect ourselves from the horror of allowing ourselves to see our horror. Perhaps essentially meaningless affairs, which the woman has no substance left to give emotion to (nor to any possible remedy for the already blankness of her existence), are other ways in which one smiles, so "she doesn't have to think."

If a tree falling is a metaphor for the damage of psychological processes, then the "sawmill" and "sawdust" are extensions that make the following thin stanza simply stunning:

In my boots, I trudge past the sawmill.
A thick paste of sawdust exposes me and coats my sweat.

Mark is a master in the use of subtle constructions, such as the application of the occasional seemingly odd word choice or the fabrication of grammar or punctuation that opens a hole to another image or meaning or modulating metaphor within an already interesting journey that is the overall poem. These layers of interwoven images are something like the seemingly confusing, yet imagination provoking and ultimately revealing color combinations or strokes in an eerie but beautiful painting. For example, in this poem the cat surprises with "Its crooked tail"; the capitalization of "Its" gives this seemingly mundane detail extra "umph", and there is indeed a crooked *tale* here - the arc of despair in crumbling lives and relationships rendered by the pathology of the lumberjack and maybe his accomplices or victims. It is not always so easy to distinguish the two. As the poet conveys,

If I believe a tree is dead already, it's easier to make wood.

Of the concept presented in the poem's last line, there could be volumes written (even physically… on the product of dead trees) in psychology books:

One by one over the felled tree, I detach its useless limbs.

To a Seamstress commemorates a mother (or another maternal figure, such as a grandmother) through the consideration of likely one of the many seemingly selfless domestic duties she performed in the care of her children (or grandchildren) through the years. Cleverly elegant, its beginning invokes the orchards and farms that provide the typically wholesome background of a Midwest upbringing ("A careful blend of favorable winds and destinations.") The perhaps not unusual sacrifice is acknowledged, as the "seamstress" truly put her blood into it; but, lurking within are hints of something grimmer. There are subtle indications that the pains endured were past the far end of the usual spectrum, with "prick" being a particularly interesting word as utilized:

Instead, the thread-drawn hands passed blood
With every prick.

It is of note that the poet and his brother Matt seem to have very different opinions as to the role that their mother played within the dysfunctional family of their childhood. Matt regards his mother as a guilty co-defendant, supporting his father's psychological dismantling of the children, actively and especially passively. In contrast, he believes that poet Mark regards his mother as being a victim, on par perhaps with the children themselves. This may have been a contributing factor, as well, to the different directions the two boys took after college. Whereas Mark apparently felt obliged to stay, including perhaps to take care of his mother (who encouraged him to stay), Matt felt that he needed to "get out" and "fix things from the outside." He specifically stated to Mark that "everyone is going to get out alive." Everyone almost did; youngest brother Michael, once diagnosed with a schizotypal personality disorder, committed suicide in April 2006.

Allowing for some personal perspective in the poem then, part of the credit for the survival of most of the progeny would seem due to the mother (or grandmother) herself. In the stanza below, the first two lines incorporate well the seamstress theme; the last two lines are particularly enriched with Mark's almost otherworldly poetic phrasing and characteristic intelligent play on words. The word "brand" can refer to the clothes from the seamstress and/or the family scar imparted from the injuries referred to above and inevitably a component of the handicaps and tools that the children must now carry on with:

So spread her grave with flowers, clipped and knitted
By their stems,
Make smooth a palette to receive
Her brand

The poem's ending allows for a level of ambiguity, in which readers can draw their own conclusions in relation to the brilliant use of symbolism reflected in "magic shovels."

*   *   *

An Anatomy Lesson in One Somnambulant Cramp, Cripples, Drug Therapy

As a physician/scientist, and one who has been forced to view things from the different perspective of a patient and particularly one with a terminal diagnosis, I especially appreciated the wisdom delivered in the poem *An Anatomy Lesson in One Somnambulant Cramp*. Science, of course, has changed everything about the world man lives in. It is unequivocally the most definitive way of knowing objective aspects of our experience, those parts that are accessible to our senses or ever-increasingly sensitive extensions of their ranges. Particularly progressively accelerating in the 20th century, the incredible success of translating scientific discoveries to useful technologies (and not so useful, as we've seen in *Elegy!*), including for creature comforts, has given a large fraction of mankind the notion that science can (… maybe eventually) explain "everything". For many scientists, materialism has essentially become as much closed-mindedly dogmatic (the "god" Cortex of Mark's poem) as some of the equally passionately held doctrines of religions that much of science feels it has successfully annihilated. However, many are increasingly recognizing that materialism is a terribly unsubstantiated and very incomplete world view[9].

Even when mechanisms for physically experienced phenomena are "known", the languages of physical or biological science (say, as in the description of muscle cramps explored in Mark's clever poem) do not always do much justice to our experience, as we actually perceive it. Many of our poet "ancestors" seem to have appreciated this all along. Fortunately, poets (unlike dogmatic scientists) don't say "I told you so!" (It's not a very poetic phrase, is it?) It's the poet's job to bitch-slap us out of the slumber of our comfortable auto-numbed minds sometimes and to "see things" (and show them to us) in ways that stretch our minds. Next time you have the pleasure of a muscle cramp, have a look at the somewhat sarcastically presented description of what's "really" happening to you in this insightful poem.

Just the title of this poem alone begins to impart a lesson in itself. The term somnambulant, of course, refers to a sleep walker. Yet, in essence, the traveler on the journey of reductionist science at the exclusion of all other experiential wisdom is just that. The more I thought on this poem, the more I see its many layers of brilliance, consciously or potentially subconsciously developed and shared. For starters, the poem itself is not particularly pleasant sounding. It is not composed of lovely words that give us pleasant sensations, though we can readily find these in Mark's other poems. That's because it is composed of the very language of its target: useful terms when interpreting an MRI, but not for cursing a cramp. Indeed, it is sleep that is the usher of dreams, with their mystifyingly complex messages from the unconscious that come to us during the period of REM sleep. This is alluded to in the first line where fishing thus in the unconscious is contrasted to that in a physical "pond". How ironic, or instructive, it is then that this potential opportunity to experience and possibly learn in dreams is interrupted by this physically described process, the cramp: the mechanistic body interfering with unconscious learning. What a good metaphor, indeed, for current societal thinking versus its need for deeper levels and broader ranges of awareness.

Cripples continues the exploration of the undesirable consequences of a purely mechanical approach by a medical profession that is based (with much success, but much residual shortcomings) upon materialist and reductionist science. As alienating as this can be to the "normal" individual, the far greater psychological devastation that such a cultural community can caustically drop upon the severely sick by its false ideals-derived projection is reflected upon here with the honesty that could only be achieved by one of the targets.

In Medieval times, cripples and other "stricken" that lay and hobbled about served as reminders of God's power and justice, a useful service provided to remind all to stay on the path ... or else[10]. Here also was a readily available opportunity to show one's virtues through acts of compassion. In our modern society, wherein we (subconsciously) expect others to play a role for us just like we play a role for them in the great drama of individual and collective ego-maintenance[11], exposure to cripples is an unwanted reminder of our own vulnerability. In a world where for many, science and the great rationality of man's mind have replaced the no-longer necessary notion of God, cripples and all the "slightly-offs" are (even if just subconsciously) a reminder of some of our persistent failures.

In *Cripples*, what could appear at first glance as essentially meaningless and unconnected illusions, bizarre ideations, and even hallucinations is actually a very informative disclosure of some of the dehumanizing aspects of the modern hospital, including specifically those portions addressing mental health, where human connection may be most important. One of the less romantic aspects of hospitals, as cleverly presented within Mark's poem, is the much higher likelihood of someone getting an infection with particularly nasty and/or particularly drug-resistant microorganisms (or "bugs"). Another is red-tape. This plague of modern society permeates all professions, but perhaps reaches its pinnacle within the health-care system and especially the hospital. Hence, we can appreciate the richly informative imagery of Mark's fantastic term, "bughouse bureaucracy", which I'm tempted to incorporate into daily conversation.

The unsettling effects that the mechanistic breakdown and reconstruction can have on the psychiatric patient (often those of richest inner content) are interestingly conveyed in:

Shiva twisting cross-legged on his pedestal-
To keep you company while you stagger to the clinic.

The undesirable "side-effects" of modern health care (not that the asylums of prior centuries were spa-holidays!) are conveyed in part in lines such as:

The walkers click or roll with the sound of ripping leather.
Like rats, they've worn themselves a maze:

Such a maze is not only the literal complex of hospital hallways, but the confusion that falls on the unsettled mind and soul of the citizen fed into the system. Yet this "valley of darkness" is what we have, with largely good intention despite a substantial ongoing degree of ignorance in so many areas of our collective civilization. And so, after the latest encounter, the poet again drums up hope...maybe it's two steps forward and only one step back, so the temporarily hospital-poisoned man moves on:

On the street he finds new appreciation
For the stability of his legs.
Yacking, clutching the prescription,
He knows he'll be better. These things take time.
Healing.

Drug Therapy also reflects on the potentially numbing effects of the more mechanical approaches of medical treatment, within the realm of that least mechanistically accessible area of psychiatry. From the insider's experience are presented some provocative poetic phrases. Layered against reference to the staggeringly complex issues of the relation between ideas and images of ideas within our head is the more practical objective of trying to get to function like everyone else the perceived individual weirdo, the one referred to in:

They liken you to a pickerel
The way your mouth opens and gawks.

Along with constituting another vivid fish analogy, the second line possibly refers to manifestations of the underlying condition or to potential uncontrolled movement and muscle tone side effects of some anti-psychotic drugs, known as extra-pyramidal symptoms.

Reflecting a recurring theme of a constrained world-view is seeing the patient as the information obtainable by physical examination:

They encapsulate an existence,
Make a study of dilated pupils.
Are my thoughts even mine anymore
   Beside the hypnotist in pill form?

Improvement in symptoms is more easily achieved now with the availability of pharmacologic treatment in schizophrenia and mood disorders by drugs that exert their beneficial effects by modulating function of amine neurotransmitters, such as dopamine and serotonin. It is thus easy (in our way of causal thinking) to blame these psychiatric conditions on primary abnormalities involved in bio-chemical regulation of these molecules. But which came first? Did some molecular changes cause the strange ideation of a schizophrenic, or did the strange ideas cause the neurotransmitter abnormalities? As expressed in utterly stunning imagery for a possible drug induced "clear-up",

   Sunspeckled break into rain
   Every hurricane embraces its eye-

perhaps we've calmed the inside turmoil. But was it the inside turmoil causing the outside symptoms, or the outside turmoil (i.e., the crazy world) causing the inside symptoms?

   Chicken or egg?

*   *   *

The spectrum of transient victories and bottomless heartbreaks associated with romantic love is perhaps the most common ingredient making up the ink in the poet's pen. But in this volume of Mark Putzi's poetry, we experience within a group of poems something different, something arguably even more tragic, in the form of poems reflecting the inability to even richly experience the grand drama to begin with. No surprise, the ego required to love securely yet openly and even humbly is an ever enriching mix of many ingredients, not a trivial source of which is one's own family. We have seen how the poet's background here could be an insurmountable handicap on the treacherous field of personal love.

Spider Song is a devastatingly haunting sketch of pathological love. Long before the internet, of course, the word "web" had been incorporated into our speech to convey the complex interconnecting elements of human society. We are held within a baffling mesh that results from the psychology of all the individual "spinners". Here, the "sinning hands" (another outstanding play on words) of an individual execute intent into the mix, encountered in phrases that remind us of the not so uncommon "free-loading" male. Once "the nest is made," in comes this seemingly likewise cursed lover "to bring his juice / injecting you with doom." The reference to impregnating sperm, another part of the mix to make a very incomplete whole, is strong here. I have entertained as well the notion of "psychological juice", the bad sort that can drain at least as much as it gives. Under these conditions, the embrace reflects an act, maybe a desperate act, more than just the physical one:

Now we embrace
My proboscis mingling
Through liquid hair.
It is a dirty job.

In this "copulation", and particularly well rendered by use of "proboscis" (a general term for a long flexible snout; or, the protruding mouth part of an insect designed for piercing and sucking), we see even more damage to the perpetually scarred players (the piercers and the pierced; the suckers and the sucked dry). The last stanza conveys something perhaps akin to what the experts may blandly present in pain-diluting terms such as "co-dependency":

We kiss good night.
The love extends to me.
Your sorrow in
Chains is my happiness.

This poet member of the scientifically gifted Putzi clan would remind us, if necessary, that arthropods analogized in *Spider Song* are quite different from the insects word played upon in the title of the poem *Insex*.

They have six legs
And segmented bodies
And when they do it
They look mechanical.

Anyone who has had both the mechanical and the more love infused and passionate non-mechanical types of sex (with either the same or different partner) would probably testify that the latter was more pleasant. But, maybe we take what we can get, and even insects have sex, says the poet's "warm" friend. This should be enough shouldn't it; after all, it's in our nature, it's instinct. Fortunately for us, the requisite acts for species propagation happen to also feel really damn good (of course, evolutionary forces have likely come into play even in this regard). Yes, let's look to see "What do their parts look like?" Surely, here is a rational approach to delivering or restoring the joys of intercourse to the damaged little biological unit the poet is. Unfortunately (or fortunately, at least when it works), the situation with humans is more complicated. Why? Maybe this friend of the poet's, who like a queen exists in her security as the little drones "hit into her," knows and can tell us. And then, the poet opens up his wound, a type that we normally don't see in the social drama in which propagate the relatively healthy, and shows us the absolute bottom: the dark cellar floor on which slink those loveless who have no choice, and for which even we, the vast blend of the normal, have no remedy for:

My friend is a therapist
I'd feel sorry for that person
If a client ever told me this
She says.

Of this small cluster of poems expressing the tragic consequences of a lover's sense of unworthiness, I placed *To Hesitate* last because of the absolute depth of the empty despair conveyed, particularly by the sense of detachment with which are presented its rather objective descriptions. Already in the first stanza there is the hint as to how the over-thinking, insecure poet has wrought his own heartbreak:

Between feeling and acting is a thought
And thoughts can make a feeling cold
So thoughts are mine but never feelings yet
A feeling unexpressed is nothing.

In the second stanza, we learn the operation and nature of wishes and notions, which may even be a source of pleasantness in periods of quiet solitude, "But notions are but thoughts again - ." Then in the last stanza, we see that this is not a philosophical discourse on cognition, but an utterance of a deepest sadness of regret because those warped thoughts prevented the actions of love, whereby the poet is constrained as "my soul sleeps." The "real" thinking, the "thinking" of the heart, is never allowed to empower action toward the truly desired end. Perhaps most tragic of all is the poet's own recognition of this gaping deficiency towards love ("knowing"-that cursed brain of thoughts again…). This awareness (politely self-regarded as a "curiosity") along with the seeming inability to do anything about it underlie the inevitability of his perpetual suffering.

What a curiosity - who I am,
I stay awake but my soul sleeps.
My heart whenever thinking of you flies
But knowing you have left me quickly dies.

*   *   *

A Painting, Building, The Jugglers, Tattoo, Bow Tie

If there is any "advantage" to growing up within a non-nurturing environment that doesn't even provide the basic infrastructure for further development of the ego[12], it is that such an individual is basically starting from scratch. He has no traces of the rules by which society's members play their interactive games[13]. This could prove variously disastrous for the vast majority of human individuals, who seek within our mainstream civilization the usual goals of fulfillment, material comfort, proper family arrangement, and status. A true seeker, even if well versed and polished in these cultural motifs, will eventually have to realize the unnatural, false, or at least woefully incomplete nature of the ego-preserving design of the daily human drama[14]. Those who are able to achieve this or who were never covered in such layers of social falsehood to begin with pay a huge price for the consequent dwelling on the outside of conventional society[15]. That costly process is shown in the poet's catalog of words and the bloody perspective from which he casts down, and all around, the darker wisdoms. Perhaps, then, the scarred poet in particular has unique insight and that is conveyed in a series of Mark's poems that could be regarded as an advanced form of "object poem"[16]. These demonstrate a sophisticated analysis derived from experience, insightful perception, deep sentiment, and longing as presented in the setting or context of a poem-titled subject.

A *Painting* contains irregular line lengths, with staggered and deeply indented line starts and abrupt terminations. Capitalizations add emphasis to key words, such as "Fall", "Golgotha" and "Jacket", as the form serves as a visual metaphor for the "Painting" that is so poignantly described in the poem. The themes of man's disconnection from nature and the tragic consequences thereof are illustrated. For example, the image of the cute little white picket fence, symbol of American suburban domestic (contained) bliss, is shattered as it becomes "the razor which impales a squirrel." With the onset of progressively reinforced methods of science and the Industrial Revolution it facilitated, man with his powerful brain and his smart-tools began to view the natural world as more of a dumb passive stage and an endless supply closet, put there for his use[17]. Mark joins a distinguished list of poets, such as Goethe and Novalis, in imparting some degree of consciousness to Nature[18]. Even though the falling ("descending innocently") leaves are not aware of time, distance, or the significance of their journey, "The ground accepts each as the caress of a hand." Could the tree in the last stanza of Mark's poem speak, would it indeed remind us again of how things may have been before we began to dismiss everything we couldn't prove by science (even if we hadn't <u>dis</u>proven it by science)? Who is it, Nature or us (a species like all else that IS part of Nature) that is "to suffer in eternity?"

A fragile and deep perspective provides the scaffolding for the sorrowful poem *Building*. Here, the poet shows us another point of view besides the day-in and day-out reality of the concrete physical world that most people are so thoroughly engaged in. Mark Putzi is clearly a master of word choice when constructing verse, such as when "timber" and "wood" are regarded as "metaphors" in contrast to the more logical regard of them as different stages or transition of material object during processing. The "metaphors" are "to differentiate / Between states of matter," wherein matter clearly indicates the physical substance of a thing, but also richly imparts the notion that things which mean something to others are not important to the poet right now, who in this case appears to be heartbroken. These lesser events ("under days and nights") can blind most of us to those things that could impact forever the inner being. In contrast, the poet's world can be changed forever by the seemingly minor detail of a passing smile. Is it that most of us are somehow removed from those life-long lasting moments of beauty, or do the average worker bees suppress their effects, even their existence, "forgetting what is lost," in order to carry on as one of "those who indifferently / Open the world to his garnered thoughts."

Wisdom-weary longing is reflected in several of Mark's poems, including *The Jugglers*. As in *A Painting*, the poet uses staggered lines within the stanzas, typically starting progressively rightward. This architecture is reminiscent of the style of some of the poems written by Mayakovsky towards the end of his short life, such as "Brooklyn Bridge" (1925), "Back Home" (1925), "Letter from Paris to Comrade Kostrov on the Nature of Love" (1928), and "At the Top of My Voice" (1930, the year of his suicide)[19] . Here, quite appropriately, the unusual style serves as a visual allegory of the very process of juggling. With reference to familiar tossed objects of the craft, the poem presents the precarious process of living, which we compartmentalize ("Separate the busy / Molecules of / Lips.") and manage at risk matched by great hope ("Like lepers do / On Christ") in careful and well-intended efforts, hoping desperately that the whole big mess doesn't come crashing down. Yet, as the wise poet reminds us, our grand plans are subject to the entropy of human chaos, just as the tossed bowling pins and bottles are to gravity. And in another clever play on words ("Were it not for / Matter, we would / Miss…"), "matter" again alludes to the physical world of matter (the juggler's objects always ready to come falling down) and the weight of meaning, those things most worth taking a "throw" on.

Tattoo and *Bow Tie* are poems that incorporate even more unique visual frameworks. These poems are reminiscent in this regard of some of Apollinaire's poems, such as "Coeur et Miroir" (with verse in the forms of a heart and a mirror); "L'oeillet" ("The Carnation", in the form of stem, leaves, and flower), and the extreme case of vertically oriented long slender columns of slightly right bending text in "Il Pleut", mimicking the very nature of its topic of raining[20].

Mark's poem *Tattoo* assumes the even more ambitious form of a butterfly, the implied design for an actual tattoo being created and received. Within the setting of a rather mundane, but most human interaction, we get a brief but intelligent commentary on the reasons we humans make and seek our rituals and symbols (from good luck charms to statues in glorious cathedrals), "The fulcrum between / Colossal good and evil." Perhaps this is all so much wishful thinking. Or, perhaps it is indeed all of the little things that are themselves the simple and real truths, colorful displays of the deepest nature of the things that seem to keep eluding our hard pondering. These are the giver and receiver moments, in which we encounter the likes of the mysticism held by the tattoo artist who "stoically transcribes" on the "intoxicated" (maybe by the usual means, which not uncommonly lowers the threshold to finally get the tattoo; or in the manner of the thirsting seeker taking action) customer's "exquisite canvas" - the skin of one who may someday truly "smile like / a Sufi." When the moment expires, the event may indeed seem like just one more regrettable empty ritual ("What have you done?"), or it may be a moment of progress to the man with the "black diamond eyes" seeing a bit more clearly that: "After all does not / a lucky man create / his own truth?"

The poem *Bow Tie* is literally in the shape of a bow tie, which provides a deeply augmenting ambience, like a stage setting for displaying a cross section of "regular people" society (the likes of whom may only ever fuss with a bow tie and gold cuff links for the handful of weddings that they are in as either groom or groomsman). In just those few self-consciously awkward moments of standing at the altar and watching the audience and proceeding participants, viscerally transmitted are thoughts and emotions that arise over lifetimes of the daily grind. Here, one gets the gut feel of a deeply transmitted story, something I have occasionally noted within the poetry of another sensitively insightful Midwesterner, James Wright (e.g., in poems like "Old Man Drunk" or "Trouble"[21]). Without overt judgment, the poem considers aspects of our culture, our traditions, even our very symbols of those things, such as the bow tie of the title.

It is interesting, and maybe somewhat ironic, how common social cycles are repeated within our micro-worlds of family, friends, workplace, and community, with each member experiencing serial aspects as he or she progresses, inexorably, in life, finding it "grotesque the speed with which time passes,..." With the best man being one of those who previously assumed the expected responsibility and the current bride and groom taking their vows in front of a group of wedding attendees who are "themselves consenting adults," we see more of the common threads between the soon to be Mr. and Mrs. and the surrounding stock from which they come and to which they contribute.

Within this progression of roles and realizations, the main conflict of the social species is presented. Perhaps it is the subconscious awareness of this that sets the austerity of this accepted participation, as indicated by the gut-wrenching and bladder loosening nervousness. Somewhere between "biological invective" (to reproduce and propagate just like any other animal, wearing bow ties or not) and the eventually learned "Richer reality of hope for generations" lies the daily life of human men and women in our current stage of biological and social evolution, for better or worse.

*　　*　　*

Seminar, Narcissus

The emotionally and psychologically expensive experiences wisely interpreted and skillfully presented in Mark's poems cannot be learned at a poetry workshop or seminar. Concentrated educational sessions may, of course, facilitate improvement in adherence to established technical aspects of writing, if that is one's objective. However, one can only live through...and hopefully endure... the severest forms of pain that some must unfortunately experience in the real world. I know, though, that the poem *Seminar* was prompted by a true experience (though I don't know the year), demonstrating if nothing else, Mark's past commitment to his work as a writer. Mark and I are both fans of the poetry of Robert Bly, the expert poet conducting the seminar, an episode of which forms the subject of this poem. Yet, the "hollow" with which Mark answers the speaker's question in the poem comes from an acquaintance with hollowness that fortunately few will have to suffer through.

Following that brief poetry spirit connection, the informal interaction that ensues in the hallway presents a potentially more universal instance, in which a more in depth exposure can be as damaging to a long-time idolized image as a discovered cover-up:

I experience

A hollowness

I'd thought unique to masks.

Mark Putzi, the poet, is always learning.

When I first met Mark, he identified himself to me as a "philosophical poet". In my possible ignorance, I don't believe this is an "official" school, past or present. It is likely more a general characterization of the mind-set and processes that shape these poems, but I believe anyone fortunate enough to read this volume will not only allow for "philosophical", but also for a whole bunch of other –"icals" as well.

Indeed, this is the required perspective for asking, "What is forgiveness?" as Mark does in the first line of the stand out poem *Narcissus*. This is a soft, but abundantly involved poem presenting a shrewd consideration of an important aspect of our interactions with others. Is forgiveness an act that out of our kindness and virtue we do others a favor by dripping a little bit of our precious oil upon them? Or, is it, possibly, "an acknowledgement that nothing exists as we believed?" After all, if everything was as we wanted it to be, nothing would ever go wrong-from within or without; the latter those things we have to forgive of others. And is it possible, in fact, that acts requiring forgiveness and especially the acts of forgiving themselves are the emotionally painful processes (those for which "We are thrice invoiced") by which we grow,

If we have courage
To initiate redemption
And avoid chicanery and the criminal Church

In the advanced vocabulary alliteration of the third line above, the poet is contrasting the painful act of forgiveness with the less personally challenging form rendered in dogmatic fashion by an essentially self-anointed authority ("God's easier softer way"). No, we are not that mythical god Narcissus looking at our grand reflection in the mirror and falling in love with ourselves. In the day-in and day-out of hurting and being hurt, and yet being able to reach deep down and learn from the hurt and the healing we give in forgiveness, we become the "anti-Narcissus", more beautiful:

Forgiveness is the language of self-love.
And we are so beautiful
Our reflections fall in love with us.

*   *   *

Fish Logic contains potent symbolism and deceptively wise metaphors in its delivery of a message that most humans simply miss, over and over again. The title itself gives pause to readers of a species that thinks so very highly of itself. Yet, we are not a finished product, certainly not as it relates to spiritual wisdom. Man is, of course, cursed not only with finitude like all living things, but especially by the awareness of such[22]. So, particularly in the Western world, we self-conceal our "absurd" situation with distractions.

> *You work all your life*
> *Make that bowl as big as possible*
> *Fish eyes rotating.*

There is also much we could still learn from one we've presumably been studying and modeling ourselves on for a long time. The symbolism of the Fish as related to Christ is more than hinted at here, as the big guy's son is named directly. Of note, however, it is the "great imagination" that "Pulled Christ up the yardarm" that is referenced for invoking, not man-made versions of increasingly meaningless dogma[23]. Amazingly large is this statement, in a philosophical sense (as one would expect from a "philosophical poet"), indicating the importance of man's imagination in development of true spiritual wholeness, an idea conveyed centuries ago by the likes of Goethe[24]. To me, the message conveyed here is more compatible with the "un-doctored up" version of the Jesus of *The Gospel of Thomas*[25], without the later added human narrative of the Canonical Gospels that has subsequently facilitated for many the dilution of Christianity into a series of rules and rituals.

If one were truly to acquire and follow Christ's wisdom, understand the message of the oneness of Nature, and have that "fish mind," instead of the insecure, death-fearing, ego-striving and hence selfish mind of the oh so superior cerebrum of the modern human being...well, maybe things wouldn't suck so bad for us... emotionally, personally, culturally, whateverly.

> *Only a mind of fish sees enormity.*
> *A fish mind is a peaceable gallows*
> *And love an earlobe you pull like a net.*

Sri Ramakrishna (who achieved Samadhi, or liberation, through a variety of disciplines including Vedanta and the message of Christ) noted, particularly towards the end of his miraculous and illustrious life, that he saw God in all things, but especially and increasingly in his fellow man[26]. How appropriate, then, including in possible relation to meditation, the incredible wisdom of the last stanza, when considering all those others that we are here with, just as scared, just as striving:

Others cold, but still breathing, breathing.
We learn of the elements
Packed against another's silence.

Swim, one of my favorite poems in this collection, offers a fresh look at experience; one that is a bit more in keeping with its raw nature and a purer approach to challenging one's self. There is a need for ego, of course, but accomplishing a mentally and/or physically demanding task, in the wild, without butchering the natural world in the process is a far healthier endeavor than, say, insulting and belittling a co-worker so that one can feel a bit better about oneself.

The natural world is, in reality, that which we are a part of and that challenges and augments us, wherein "we dive into cold" and the body of water faced and submerged in "boils and resists." There is a sense of the sacred or of a ritual act here, perhaps even a connecting to wetness. This feeling of partnership with the more primal is communicated in wonderful phrasing:

And you've a stomach of sea water
To drive your muscles.

Here we see fish as fish, interacting with and responding to the swimmer...as fish...not as a branch on a man-made classification scheme, that very narrowly focused human world generated from a need for control, from our science, from our conveniently conceived of gods, whereby we derive our frequently invoked "authority". Appropriately indicated within the water milieu:

They can't bend to your ordered ruling
Between Neptune and Zeus.

In *Underwater Sketches*, the verse paints images harmonious to the meditative spirit. While we focus so hard on the material world presented to our senses and incorporating more and more human-derived information, we run the risk of not noting even the manifested aspects of a great unity; a oneness that includes also everything that has come before. It is in the here and now that each item and each experience carries the code of a universal presence. Music, in particular of all man's achievements, may best capture the abstract nature of a universal harmony. How wise, then, it is to block the input of our everyday ears, and let the even deeper music, of which we are a part, come to the fore:

> *How clear the music comes to us through the water in our ears*
> *And how blest are we to know only the song and not its history.*

My wife Heidi is an avid scuba diver. If you ask her why she dives, she will say that the main reasons are to get away from the chaos of everyday life and to get into a setting where one can experience a vast other world, as "…is the ocean itself not treasure?" A further objective in pursuing deeper and deeper diving is the reaching of almost absolute silence and a darker and ever more peaceful world, a place utterly perfect for a contemplative experience. Mark creates such a setting to help us learn to just be, to experience our fundamental relation to other aspects of creation, and to delve ever deeper:

> *I ply myself and am abandoned*
> *Mutually to exist.*
> *The many types of anamalia*
> *Bead against the shallow skin*
> *The bubble that we see.*
> *But always another layer peeled*
> *Becomes darker and darker*
> *Until at last our eyes are useless*
> *And we see only with our souls*
> *And measure time against our pulses*
> *And deepen into the incomprehensible silence*

Many religions offer ritualistic formulas intended to confer unverifiable immortality. For the mystical sages, it is when you truly realize that you are ONE with all things that you are free from death; you are immortal. How could you be otherwise? Unless one has been to this "place", there are no words (inventions of man) that can convey this. It is a hard way; related to, but bigger even than obtaining psychological wholeness, which is hinted at here by reference to Anima and Animus. There are also other elements within the poem's underwater setting that may be encountered in Jungian psychology, such as the dark, evil, female one being the missing element in the Christian Trinity and/or representing an unconscious element needed for psychological wholeness[27]. Yet, Mark may be striving to take us still further, as even a whole man is but a small part:

> ...*we who had been anima and*
> *Animus...a scratch on the*
> *Surface of the pearl, black*
> *And consummate as night*

At this point the line style of the poem itself changes, in parallel with the transformation reflected in the verse. We are reminded (as per the seers of Eastern mysticism) that what it is we seek, we CANNOT know by our intelligence. This can be a hard mouthful of salt water to swallow.

> *And if there's knowing it's apart from us*

Instead, we are provided with something more like an existentialist call to strive on anyway:

> *To quietly proceed*
> *Fear and bravery feeding each other*

How profound that concept of synergy between two attributes typically regarded as mutually exclusive in our over-simplified relative view of the world! In Whitmanesque simple to the point beauty[28], if there is death, it gives rise to birth:

> *And like worms*
> *Wearing each other's skin*
> *There is a resolution in the souls*
> *For March and its annual return*
> *Quiet only*
> *The leaves ache to be borne*
> *The wind to bear*
> *And you and I*
> *To be.*

I will keep this one close at hand, as I move closer for "The wind to bear" my ashes. Thanks Mark.

Mark's call for us to awaken to a true knowledge and a richer humanity is expressed most vehemently in *Daylight*. This apocalyptic rant rich with psychedelic imagery illustrates several of the elements that I particularly appreciate in his poetry. One is, again, the clever play on words, including through the birth of neologisms that add the texture of possible multiple meanings or complex flavorings:

> *When lack of sleep forces open*
> *The cavern of misering thoughts*

The word "misering" adds depth and convolutions to our thoughts being referred to; those we hold tightly in our caves as a *miser* may (like Scrooge with his money) and those that impart *misery*, a property we may not be aware of. Neologisms put Mark in good company, along with the likes of Whitman, Rimbaud, and Corso, in addition to Mayakovsky. When the crappy state of man in his ego-guided society needs a cerebral enema, a new voice is needed, and the old language is sometimes just not quite adequate for the expression of the required purging ideas.

Also, the allowance for objects to have a degree of consciousness adds to the layers of psychological and philosophical depth. Although these things may be far less capable of specific functions that we hold so dear (such as thinking and free will), we humans haven't exactly used such supposedly higher states of mind to ascend to a level meriting a gold star. For example, in a slight reference to the dread-imposing pronouncement of "the bell tolls for thee," we have in the next two lines both an object with knowledge and an indication of a nasty practice of humans, a blight that lingers on its own accord:

> *And the bell knows its wind and*
> *Echoes from enslavement, …*

Another feature of Mark's poetry, also predicated on his high level of intelligence, is the incorporation of frames of reference given by phrases noting bits of science, history, and literature. In the second stanza, cell memory could be a property (even consistent with emerging broader views of science) of the "tail" tissues of the imprisoned organisms. It could also refer to the tragic recall of the prison cells themselves (as per object consciousness noted above), in which "tails" can serve as "tales", those of the horrid experiences recalled by the victims of the old ways, the ways symbolized by the "Busts of the Greeks and torturers." The sophistication of this element in Mark's poetry is well illustrated in the adroit maneuvers with the lives and works of science icons Galileo and Newton, wherein objects of gravity testing (say, like balls that could be dropped off the tower of Pisa) call attention to aspects of human kind (e.g., "balls" that could be testicles, of Newton in this case, as the familiar slang for courage or conviction). All this in a sentence within the last five lines that, while staying faithful enough to the historical tale of apples falling on Newton's head in a gravity-inspiring moment, possibly implicates a major source of all that man-made knowledge (the "papers" in the storm); that is, the entity that paradoxically gives us the story of the tree of knowledge yet threatens the head (and more than just threatened that of others) of one of mankind's greatest thinkers:

And whatever it is we knew emptied
Out. And the storm feathered its
Night with papers. And the tree of
Knowledge dropped fruit on Newton's
Balls and Galileo's head, and again
We saw it torn down what we made
When sleepless eyelids pried apart.

*   *   *

The Lover as Poet, To a Young Poet with Writer's Block

In contrast to the poet selflessly expressing subconscious truths gained as a consequence of his own experiences and strivings, the "false poet" using his craft for personal gain and ego reinforcement is indicted in *The Lover as Poet*. Given the time-immemorial use of poetry to express romantic desire, one may question how we could regard the lover as a false poet. Well, there's romantic love, of course, a laudable end for humans in general; but then again, there's also just trying to get laid:

The little girls must be impressed to spread
Their legs, so he writes with confidence

This is likely the confidence that comes with a defined purpose; the attitude that must be assumed to be "successful". Though "working diligently, perfecting each / Concept and image" may be admirable if applied sincerely to a worthwhile end, here it incriminates the one who uses his skills and status to just secure more of that status, that effort symbolized in the interesting break in "reaches" immediately following in the second stanza:

> *...he morbidly reach-*
> *Es, then stoops to insert it anally*

"Anally" may refer to compulsiveness or perfectionism, which one so determined to use his craft to achieve an aim may "insert" into his effort, but it is also the compromise of the false poet, bending over and "taking it in the ass"-in a symbolic sense. When the sleazy word-crafter for panty-invasion "subjects himself to these procedures" it is an unnatural process focused on short term material gain, compared to the searching and soul-reinforcing efforts of the true artist, who like Mark, would never sincerely compose "Lines to make the angels bear false witness."

When a true poet writes a love poem, he expresses real potencies from within his true self and is not capable of making false statements only for personal gain in non-heartfelt pursuits. As Mark informs us at the beginning of *To a Young Poet with Writer's Block*:

> *That thing in you that wants to say will not be long silent.*
> *Young women have a way of reckoning with words*
> *But never forcefully. ...*

This is a poem laced with magical phrases showing how the real poet gives from himself that which needs expressing, that which burns his heart and soul, like an addicting and craved drug; that is the energy, be it pain of experience or pain of longing or love, which gives birth to true art and carries it outward:

> *Syllables heating behind your countenance*
> *About to boil are not the tongue of a sword,*
> *But of a hypodermic needle, ready to inject*
> *What murders from within: ...*

In essence, the writer's block of youth is the relative lack of experience of these human interactive dynamics; the cumulative heartbreaks, disappointments, beat downs, and risings that teach one to give of oneself and to take from others that which is extended in a true dance of humanity. The non-young poet seeks the "returning sigh," and he can give all his inner "quiet torments," no matter what was their cost. He must "step," which is the emotional and spiritual process of writing the poem:

...like one oppressed I
Feel my heart's excessive weight and step to bring its fall.

*   *   *

Grievance, Bio

Over the years, particularly after the period of his most severe bouts with mental illness, Mark had contemplated pursuing professions compatible with his scientific interests. It should come as no surprise that in these endeavors Mark received parental resistance rather than support. When I first met Mark and received several of his already composed poems in January 2011, he was starting his last semester of Pharmacy school, which he had begun at the University of Wisconsin in Madison back in 2007. Now, in order to save money Mark had returned to Milwaukee in January 2011 so as to complete his remaining clinical rotations while being able to live again in his parents' home.

Commensurate with his obvious intelligence and notable diligence, Mark had been doing very well in his program on his way to a doctorate of pharmacy degree; an A student and clearly on the "home stretch". In "home", though, may literally be one possible problem. As I was communicating with Mark regarding obtaining more poems for possible inclusion in this volume, I learned from Matt that Mark had failed one of his clinical rotations in Milwaukee. Subsequent details indicated that he was attempting a complex clinical rotation at the very same hospital at which he had been sick enough to be in and out of the locked wards for six years, from age 33 to 39 years old. Returning to these props and settings of his own past nightmare could be regarded either as a self-imposed extreme challenge to allow for some sort of final victory or unequivocal expression of healing; or as Matt regarded it, a subconscious act of self-sabotage. Following the F-bomb experienced upon grade day, Mark was then even refusing to work with the Pharmacy school officials regarding other options towards successful program completion.

Brother Matt suspected that under these adverse conditions, our poet hero may have been off his medications and lodged in a familiar defiant posture, which would include the propensity to blame others and a refusal of any "outside" assistance (particularly of the personal/familial variety). Yet, Mark assured us that the above noted possible personal challenges had nothing to do with his failing grade. Instead, he ascribed it primarily to the more straightforward factor that his preceptor was an "asshole". In the meantime, my ability to be a pest was rewarded not only by the provision of many additional poems written in the past, but by three newly written poems, two of which are included at the end of this collection. When Mark sent the new poems, he commented that he had attempted to write like Mayakovsky would, but that he believed he had failed. Noting that these siblings have a particularly harsh scale by which they assess their own achievements (and little wonder as to why), I thought that in addition to examining the poems on their own merits, I would also try to decide whether his goal had been achieved. Well, after all of this, not only do I consider the last two poems a good place to leave things at this stage, I also believe that if Vladimir himself were looking down, he would give a sinister grin of pleased recognition and even rare approval.

In ultimately facing his pharmaceutical tribune within the poem *Grievance*, the poet (let's go ahead and allow this one to be at least somewhat autobiographical), already one strike down, must go up against the "infinite" (the designated, as suspect, wisdom of the dean) and the "Epic" (the computer system, also partly implicated for the student's failure). In capitulating to the authority one contributing factor at a time, the poet/pharmacist-wannabe arrives in an all too familiar dark hole; it is almost mythological that this latest descent is actually in the same past accomplice hospital:

…You have / Failed. You are a failure. …

Then a few lines further along, in something past ironic, something deeper than understatement, the "worthless / Shit" is told:

We hope you learn from this experience.

Are you kidding?! This one's been learning for more than four decades from every experience encountered as an opportunity to be squashed as a failure:

… I have been a shit before, no doubt
Will be a shit again, …

It is perhaps an interesting side note of further correlation that although not much is known about the poet Mayakovsky's childhood, motifs noted in his poetry include a father often portrayed in terrifying images along with anguished appeals to his mother[29]. As to the targeted nature of Mayakovsky poetry, such self-deprecation in this current poem may not seem to compare well with the usual self-aggrandizement evident in the verse of this past seemingly egomaniac Russian[30]. We have already speculated that the almost god level position he gave himself in verse may have been assumed in order just to serve, and the true hidden sense of self-worth could have been more similar to that conveyed here, in this poem and in this whole collection. Regardless of the truth of these two possible extremes, the second half of the second stanza shows that the current poet, like the cited emulated predecessor, has no problem dishing out his intellectually confident judgments. We have an "asshole" preceptor, a dean still loitering "in her infinite wisdom," and three others making judgments on "hearsay." And, enough is finally enough:

Though the dean's decision is final that doesn't make it right.

Mayakovsky's ability to attack and destroy weaker souls falling within the targets of his self-anointed authority were and are well recognized[31]. Yet, in the late 1920s, he clearly recognized how short the new Soviet regime was compared to the ideal that he had given so very much of himself in the service of its establishment and maintenance. Woefully disillusioned by what he had helped wrought, he responded, appropriately, in the fashion he was best suited for; that is, in the form of art. Far from career (or survival) enhancing in the emerging atmosphere of the time, he composed *The Bedbug* in 1928, "one of the most devastating satires of communist society in contemporary literature[32]." This showed once more his selfless dedication to serving the people, and his ability to unabashedly present his "grievance", without regard to the potential consequences. As the dark phases of Stalin's purges ushered in the exile and/or execution of many of Mayakovsky's poet colleagues, the political writing was on the wall, and the poet took his own life on April 14, 1930 by losing at his third hand of playing Russian roulette[33].

In Mark's *Grievance*, he is expressing, at long last, "No! I do no longer recognize this type of authority." This is so, whether it be the authority of the Dean of Pharmacy or the Dean of the family. "Please sign and date this document and return it to me."

In the last poem, a hypersensitive flight of ideas, I think we can also allow for some autobiographical reference; after all, it is called *Bio*. Many complex philosophical, psychological, and sociological comments are embedded within this life-paralleling poem. Within the "longer, busier, / Convoluted – Out of my control" tale, there are bluntly expressed frustrations (as also noted particularly in some of Mayakovsky's early work) directed against the stifling nature of academia and/or the system in charge:

> ...*The Chairman,*
> *His nemesis, wasn't only going*
> *To kill him, but kill and eat him. ...*

Reflected upon by the young, hopeful, but open-eyed poet is our society's lack of brains, balls, and/or other necessary parts to do anything more meaningful towards true progress than simply sitting around and gaping at the horror. In the context of the narrator/author beginning another novel,

> ...*--About delivering*
> *Pizzas, an autobiography, one*
> *To the CNN van during Jeffrey*
> *Dahmer's trial – He said the hearts tasted*
> *Like steak - ...*

we catch a glimpse of a collective social psychology that utterly baffles the largely removed observer, one whose sensitivity is matched by a propensity towards logic and objective thinking. Unfortunately, similar examples of a collectively insane society can be pulled from the news every single day. Within the information explosion era we live in, we are bombarded with largely ignored lip service from well-wishers impotent or unwilling to do anything substantial towards a greater collective spiritual good. And we especially don't want anyone uniquely sensitive (those who can't seem to fit in and that WE find so "abnormal") indicating to us how fucked up WE are. No, these loonies, these poets, need to be locked up, as they clearly don't get it; just listen to the strange crap they utter and scribble. But who indeed are the real mad men?

As Mayakovsky wrote:

> *On the pavement*
> *of my trampled soul*
> *the steps of madmen*
> *weave the prints of rude crude words.*[34]

Poet Mark Putzi is telling us something about our society and the lives we carve out within its constraints and oblivions. But, we see where it got Mark, at least in the first round or two:

> *...And later, turning to poems.*
> *Changing my career, but still having to*
> *Write, and publications coming faster*
> *Until finally the book was finished*
> *And so was I until I turned to drugs.*

Rescued (perhaps) by sobriety, pharmacology, and complimentary modern medical programs and being steadily restored (hopefully) such that he can play his multiple roles in a wished for better world, Mark completed his Pharmacy degree and made his way steadily through the certification exam process. We'll see how it goes. I for one hope to be around for a little while at least, in part so I can read and learn more from the great poetry that comes from Mark's beautiful mind. His great brain would be an unfair competitive advantage...if it weren't for all those pesky feelings...if he could just be more of a "shit".

peace
scotT (small component of the Total)

Scott B. Shappell, M.D., Ph.D.
From Somewhere Over England
November 2011, March 2012

Notes

1) Scott B. Shappell, *I Reach Over. Poems and Spiritual Correspondences on ALS, Death, and Living*, with Sally F. Kilpatrick, Katy Rigler, Simon Hayward, M. Scott Lucia, and Stanley H. Appel; Hekaśa Publishing, Dallas, TX, 2010; pages 156, 162.

2) *Vladimir Mayakovsky: The Bedbug and Selected Poetry*, edited with an introduction by Patricia Blake, translated by Max Hayward and George Reavey; Indiana University Press, Bloomington, Indiana, 1975.

3) Ibid. pages 190-207; poem translated by George Reavey.

4) Diane Morgan, *The Best Guide to Eastern Philosophy and Religion*; Renaissance Books, Los Angeles, 2001; Thomas Merton, *Zen and the Birds of Appetite*, New Directions, 1968; Fritjof Capra, *The Tao of Physics*, Bantom First Edition, 1975.

5) Carl Gustav Jung, "On the Relation of Analytical Psychology to Poetry", in *The Spirit in Man, Art, and Literature, The Collected Works of C.G. Jung, Volume 15*, edited by H. Read, M. Fordham, G. Adler, and W. McGuire, translated by R.F.C. Hull; Princeton University Press, 1971; pages 65-83.

6) Israel Rosenfield, *The Invention of Memory. A New View of the Brain*; Basic Books, Inc., New York, 1988; pages 6, 75-80, 157-158.

7) "OM" (pronounced and/or symbolized as "A-U-M"; A as the mother-sound, naturally uttered by every creature when the throat and mouth are opened; M as the termination of speaking when the lips are closed; U as the sound when the "A" is carried to the "M"), in reference to God-realization; *Katha Upanishad* I. ii. 15 - in *The Upanishads*, translated with commentary by Swami Paramananda; Axiom Books, 2004; pages 47-48.

8) Sylvia Plath, *The Collected Poems*, edited and with an introduction by Ted Hughes, Harper Perennial Modern Classics, New York, 2008; pages 64-65. ("The Thin People" written in 1957 was originally published in Sylvia Plath's *The Colossus;* London 1960, New York 1962.)

9) For example, see Bernard Haisch, Ph.D., *The God Theory. Universes, Zero-Point Fields, and What's Behind It All*; Weiser Books, 2006.

10) A well-recognized example is how beggars and cripples (*"cour des miracles"*) are presented in the art of Hieronymus Bosch (~1450-1516); see Sandra Orienti and René de Solier, *Hieronymus Bosch*, Crescent Books, New York, 1976 (or specific works such as *Temptations of St. Anthony* or *The Cripples* on line); or history references, such as Andrew McCall, *The Medieval Underworld*, Trafalgar Square, 1979.

11) Ernest Becker, *The Birth and Death of Meaning. An Interdisciplinary Perspective on the Problem of Man*. Second Edition; The Free Press, New York, 1971 (original ©, 1962).

12) C.G. Jung, "The Stages of Life", translated by R.F.C. Hull, - in *The Portable Jung*, edited by Joseph Campbell, Penguin Books, New York, 1971; pages 3-22.

13) Becker, *The Birth and Death of Meaning.*

14) C.G. Jung, "The Stages of Life"; E. Becker, *The Birth and Death of Meaning*, pages 145-146.

15) C.G. Jung, "On the Relation of Analytical Psychology to Poetry", pages 301-322; Colin Wilson, *The Outsider*, The Riverside Press, 1956.

16) Robert Bly, *News of the Universe. Poems of Twofold Consciousness*, Sierra Club Books, San Francisco, 1980; pages 210-214.

17) ibid. pages 8-17.

18) Ibid. pages 30-37.

19) P. Blake, in introduction to *Vladimir Mayakovsky: The Bedbug and Selected Poetry*, page 9.

20) *Guillaume Apollinaire: Selected Writings*, translated with a critical introduction by Roger Shattuck, New Directions Books, New York, 1948; pages 167, 169, 171.

21) James Wright, *Above the River. The Complete Poems*, Farrar, Straus and Giroux and University Press of New England (Wesleyan Press Edition); pages 51, 193.

22) Albert Camus, "The Myth of Sisyphus", in *The Myth of Sisyphus: And Other Essays*, Vintage International, 1991 (© 1955, Alfred A. Knopf). (To Camus, man's finitude and his awareness of that mortality constitute an absurd reality, and the only true philosophical problem for man is suicide).

23) For example, see C.G. Jung, "Introduction to the Religious and Psychological Problems of Alchemy", in *Psychology and Alchemy, The Collected Works of C.G. Jung, Volume 12*, edited by H. Read, M. Fordham, G. Adler, and W. McGuire, translated by R.F.C. Hull; Princeton University Press, 1968; page 16.

24) Gary Lachman, "In the Goethe Archives", in *Rudolf Steiner. An Introduction to His Life and Work*, Jeremy P. Tarcher / Penguin, New York, 2007; pages 95, 97; Christopher Middleton, Introduction to *Johann Wolfgang von Goethe, Selected Poems (Goethe's Collected Works, Volume 1)*, edited by C. Middleton, Princeton University Press, 1994.

25) *The Gospel of Thomas*, translated and annotated by Stevan Davies, Skylight Paths Publishing, Woodstock, Vermont, 2002. (*The Gospel of Thomas* was possibly written by an actual companion of the living Jesus, decades to centuries before the canonical gospels, multiple of which appear to borrow portions from its contents, in addition to imposing their own author's purposeful narrative.)

26) *The Gospel of Sri Ramakrishna*, Abridged Edition, translated with introduction by Swami Nikhilananda, Ramakrishna-Vivekananda Center, New York, 1942 (Seventh Printing 2005).

27) C.G. Jung, "Concerning the Archetypes, with Special Reference to the Anima Concept", in *The Archetypes and the Collective Unconscious, The Collected Works of C.G. Jung, Volume 9, Part 1*, edited by H. Read, M. Fordham, G. Adler, and W. McGuire, translated by R.F.C. Hull; Princeton University Press, 1969; pages 54-72; "A Psychological Approach to the Dogma of the Trinity (Part 5: The Problem of the Fourth)", in *Psychology and Religion: West and East, The Collected Works of C.G. Jung, Volume 11, Second Edition*, edited by H. Read, M. Fordham, G. Adler, and W. McGuire, translated by R.F.C. Hull; Princeton University Press, 1969; pages 164-192; "Individual Dream Symbolism in Relation to Alchemy (Chapter 3: The Symbolism of the Mandala)", in *Psychology and Alchemy*, pages 112, 115, 120, 123, 150-151, 152, 162, 196.

28) For example: "And these one and all tend inward to me, and I tend outward to them, / And such as it is to be of these more or less I am." Or - "And as to you corpse I think you are good manure, but that does not offend me, / I smell the white roses sweetened and growing, / I reach to the leafy lips .... I reach to the polished breasts of melons, / And as to you life, I reckon you are the leavings of many deaths, / No doubt I have died myself

ten thousand times before." Walt Whitman, *Leaves of Grass. The First (1855) Edition*, edited with introduction by Malcolm Cowley, Penguin Classics, 1986; pages 40, 84.

29) P. Blake, page 14.

30) Ibid. page 15. (For example, when he was in prison for pro-Bolshevik activities in 1908 at age 15, Mayakovsky read substantially including "disposing of" contemporary authors as well as "plunging" into Shakespeare, Byron, and Tolstoy. As he communicated in his autobiography, cited by Blake, "The authors I had read were the so-called great ones, but how easy to write better than they!")

31) Ibid. pages 27-29. (Mayakovsky's ability to express his "grievances" against others included, for example, his notorious attack on recently dead poet Sergei Esenin in a cruel poem regarding the latter's suicide in 1925. In Mayakovsky's 1926 "How to Make Verse", he claimed that his aim was "to deliberately paralyze the action of Esenin's last lines"… "For the working class needs strength in order to continue the revolution which demands …that we glorify life and the joy that is to be found along that most difficult of roads – the road towards communism.")

32) Ibid. pages 37-40. (*The Bedbug* was actually produced and presented in a public theater shortly after its composition. It was not well received, perhaps partly due to its avant garde production style. As Mayakovsky's position was still fairly secure in 1928, critics did not attack it openly. Decades later, Mayakovsky's play was appreciated much more by the Russian population that had endured the Stalin era; but of course, the author was long gone by then.)

33) Ibid. page 9.

34) From the poem "I", *Vladimir Mayakovsky: The Bedbug and Selected Poetry*, edited by P. Blake; pages 52-59. Poem translated by George Reavey. (Note: After all of this, Mark says that he did fail, as he "couldn't write with Mayakovsky's confidence.")

```
i a t n e l f i s h l o g i c a v e r s t a y d o g k c u l
n j c o r s e t a o l w o b a p a n a t e n a r c i s s u s
s c u b a p e a l w a p s e n a p a n t n e s s a t v i s s
o x n g u s e a m s t r e s s w a p a i n t i n g r n o t t
m u d o t o m o o n e i l t w r i e t l o f t o w r e a l h
t h e t h f e l l e d c p l l e s s o n i n o n e u r d y e
h s r o i t r u d g e k p a m m s o m n a m b u l a n t c l
e i w s n r k m m p u d a y a h o m y s n o i t c u d e r f
j d a s l u h b o y k n o w s w o o d a y l i g h t o r a i
u a t t i b c e o f u n c o o l i e t d p e e l s a b o m r
g g e o m e t r y n a n t i b i o t i c s e p a a i y c p b
g o r o b l o j u g g l c l i p s d w o b l e s n l i k k r
l l s i s y b a b b e s t l m a n y o r u b b i g u e s s i
e i k a e s m c e w o i m d e w e t r t y s g h e a d a t s
r p e a c e u k e w l a e l x s t d u e p t h e l o v e r k
s s t i l a v a n c o m y c o a m u f x o b o a s p o e t e
x t c a s m e n s u c k h m t o b e b e e r o r r p t p o t
i c h r n u r d r z o d s p i d e l x l m s u t g i r l s a
a v e r y r o w e t u n w p c c g i l i s n a n r k a l p s
t e s o a d d i c t h e i r i a a g l g c r u w c n w o r s
g r s w w e p f r a n i m e s r d y a y g o h o g o s g e l
o s l b o r e e i l b l a c k e s t f o y t l u n a i g a e
o e e s l i p u p e n a l g b f g l o a i b a h t g u r d o
d w e p o e m l p i l l s u t u r r o w p g l e r u l i a f
t o f i i v x o l a e h e r r l i t i d e m u r e b d e a n
r n b d d l i d e n i c i d e m t l s e e l c h x i f v a n
a l f e e l f l s c h i c k e n t o d a v w h i g o t a n F
e m p r r y p a r e h t g u r d o o w i i a r e a p e n e u
h y e s o n g h t g i n s e x d o i t i n r n j a z z c a n
e t a t i s e h o g u a l s t o l e e h w g o c o d i e l k
```

Poems

My Uncle's Mexico

Its windows are but indicators the entire country is opaque.
Flies dance on their panes, and in his mines opals ruminate
On becoming diamonds. The president is not a gringo
But the head of a democracy as old as Villa Poncho.

Indicate to me the vast island of Tiajuana, and 2000 miles
Of driving in an old white Chevy, the piñata ensconced behind
You in its pile of rubbish: sombreros, stick puppets,
Jars of washed and unwashed opals, and candy made from the reduction

Of juiced papayas. Al, you impressed your ten-year-old nephew
With otherworldly knowledge, with stories of a nation-wide
Siesta. You stopped in Texas long enough to drop off
Your dark girlfriend at her cousin's. You connected your casual love

Of Wisconsin with infrequent journeys, dragging your skin
To where as a boy I thought, "My God! I've Spanish kin."

Elegy

Everyone who saw this
Wrote a poem in their heads
As soon as it happened.
It's the way we remember.

And then to see again and again
For many days thereafter:
It was like multiple surgeries
Of the same resected bowel.

I remember my brother's face
As he described and concluded,
"We're at war," and Deb due
In two months saying,

"All I give a fuck about is this baby."
And I described not feeling
And the wait began for our response,
And the debate over ethical correctness.

And I wondered what cry
Did their souls send up
Into the imperious heavens,
The many thousand dead at once?

Hear it sounding over and over,
In the shrill night, between the
Blades of my fan in searing
Summer, the Everlasting Om?

And the sound of justice
In reply, the thunderbolt
Thrown down and down again
By American Zeus? Now we know

What it was like for Japan in '45
Hit not once but twice.

Addict

The quiet man descends, having awakened
In himself a certain intellectual curiosity,
And holding a saber poised to shoulder strike,
Whispers with his feet until the man
Who has so terrified him discovers
The blade just before the fracturing of skull.
The one left standing contemplates the meandering
Circus of his fears, and with a rational leap
Expounds upon the rightness of his kill.
"Whatever doesn't kill me can only hospitalize me,"
He resolves, quoting line and text from a butcher's
Manual on ethics, and the California State Penal Code.
Licking his stained fingers, then resolving abstinence,
He prowls above his crouched shadow of lead.

Lumberjack and Wife

My whole life I've studied geometry.
Who besides me understands where a tree will fall?

A woman cries and says she feels guilty
Everything must be reduced to its elemental state.

Between the vertical and the horizontal is a crashing arc of moaning limbs.
I with my saw carefully place its descent.

At home her lover muses as she smokes and feigns indifference.
The house is paid for. The children are at school. The money's in the bank.

In my boots, I trudge past the sawmill.
A thick paste of sawdust exposes me and coats my sweat.

She waters the plants, fries two eggs and looks out the window.
The cat surprises her with Its crooked tail. Smiling again, she doesn't have to think.

I capture the first rays of sunlight through the mountain.
If I believe a tree is dead already, it's easier to make wood.

She disposes of the tissue heavy with her crying.
In all the world there's only me, she thinks, none other I can trust.

She reads for fifteen minutes, then contemplates the soiled bed sheets.
One by one over the felled tree, I detach its useless limbs.

To A Seamstress

Apples bloom, grow fat and depart in shriveled loads
A careful blend of favorable winds and destination:
Rows of corn swept by a combine, a flight of crows.

She made

Charlotte's corset,
A suit for my Confirmation,
Fifty pleats for Mary's wedding dress,
And a million stitches between the lot of us.

Suppose, instead of nothing, we had each been charged
A year for her work. Our youth worn but little
Would have shielded her from frosts.

Instead, the thread-drawn hands passed blood
With every prick.

So spread her grave with flowers, clipped and knitted
By their stems,
Make smooth a palette to receive
Her brand.

Soon we'll know by only this who tailored us
And passed down
Needles,

Who bent to make us a children who'd believe
We'd lay down
Our marvelous shovels.

An Anatomy Lesson in One Somnambulant Cramp

REM phase......fishing in the pond that never existed behind Uncle Lloyd's farmhouse
(from which he moved seventeen years ago, then subsequently died)

Suddenly plantar flexion...consciousness...
Gastrocnemeus has gone to total tetany
Phalanges flexed
Suggesting synergy of soleus...

"Do I elevate the leg?"
Involving sartorius, gracillus,
Rectus femorus and other quads?
"The only answer," concludes Cortex.

Grasp metacarpals with phalanges
Force dorsiflexion using deltoids
Trapezii, latissimus dorsi, teres
Majors and Minors
Rhomboids and others...

"Relaxation phase......Ah!!!!!"
Now tibius anterior responds
And the foot dorsiflexes on its own.
"Be careful," says Cortex, "until"

Gastrocnemius relaxes completely,
Free nerve endings register
A dull persistent ache.
"Don't let go just yet."

Eyes encapsulating a visual field
Lenses focusing... "It's time to get
Out of bed
And wash (epidermis)."

Cripples

Ball bearing eyes, zipper mouths,
Channel lock hands, brain stems
Yanked from F-150 drive trains,
And motor oil for blood.

Like an experimental aircraft, one from which the pilot is
More than ready to eject, he arches downward,
Trumpets over a gum wrapper.

The flu virus welcomes him.
"Here's a nice hallucination—
Shiva twisting cross-legged on his pedestal—
To keep you company while you stagger to the clinic.

And we paint him the color of storms."

His profile a map of industrialized Europe,
He grimaces at questions smilingly posed
By the receptionist; bughouse bureaucracy.

Insurance? Never!
Is October the month of Nemesis? Yes.
What did John Glenn do in order to vomit in space? I don't know.

The walkers click or roll with the sound of ripping leather.
Like rats, they've worn themselves a maze:
Countenances of mottled caulk.
An ER full of broken arms and
Family discussion.
The janitor's bucket squeaks the hallway marathon, controlled
By a mop handle.

For $100 anyone can walk this valley of darkness.

On the street he finds new appreciation
For the stability of his legs.
Yacking, clutching the prescription,
He knows he'll be better. These things take time.
Healing.

Drug Therapy

Idea placed into head
Appears suddenly on screen.
So which came first?
           The question no one can answer.

They liken you to a pickerel
The way your mouth opens and gawks.
The spiral of the sky opens up
           And the vortex of clouds.

And underneath its history,
The shadows convalesce as well.
When we sleep there are pictures on the walls:
           Four hundred novel pages left.

They encapsulate an existence,
Make a study of dilated pupils.
Are my thoughts even mine anymore
           Beside the hypnotist in pill form?

Sleep is contagious at night
But working diligently, painting,
My friend sitting up awake
           Knows sleep as well: It's Haldol.

And we are friends.
Idea placed into head.
So which came first?
           Sunspeckled break into rain
           Every hurricane embraces its eye-
Chicken or egg?

Spider Song

Your sinning hands
Tirelessly in the web
Collect its love
Making everything yours.

Your lover waits
Until the nest is made
To bring his juice
Injecting you with doom.

Now we embrace
My proboscis mingling
Through liquid hair.
It is a dirty job.

We kiss good night.
The love extends to me.
Your sorrow in
Chains is my happiness.

Insex

They have six legs
And segmented bodies
And when they do it
They look mechanical.

My friend finds them
Down there and warm
Herself thinks, Yes!
They do it, even insects!

Why then don't I
She thinks and she begins.
What do their parts look like?
She strains to see.

And then she flies in air
And the drones hit into her.
Left and right they fly.
Absolute she lives.

My friend is a therapist.
I'd feel sorry for that person
If a client ever told me this
She says.

To Hesitate

Between feeling and acting is a thought
And thoughts can make a feeling cold
So thoughts are mine but never feelings yet
A feeling unexpressed is nothing.

I wish myself the finest things in life
Spend my life pertained to wishing,
In quiet thoughts the notions bless me still
But notions are but thoughts again –

What a curiosity – who I am,
I stay awake but my soul sleeps.
My heart whenever thinking of you flies
But knowing you have left me quickly dies.

A Painting

In the foreground two mourning doves stand back to back, like a pair of dueling men,
But the space between them measures instead their indifference to each other.

The people know those leaves are really reeds and they walk the path of Jesus
      Through Jerusalem where the wedding party sets its feast and on to
                                    Golgotha. One

Man stands closer than the others, his hands in his pockets, proud of his red
                                          Jacket.

To his left is the razor which impales a squirrel, a picket white fence separating
      Mankind from everything in Nature
                          Except for leaves which descend innocently
                        Every Fall

Knowing neither time,
        Nor distance,
                Nor the significance of their mournful flight.

They are orange and green and trees shape them and make them beautiful
      Before letting them go.
                The ground accepts each as the caress of a hand.

In the extreme right foreground, a gray mourning dove roosts
                Contemplatively gazing,
      The thing it knows cannot be expressed.

And the trees are stalwart.
        If I break off a limb perhaps one will speak
        Of what it was to live before the Age of Reason
        And what it is to suffer in eternity.

Building

They are building now
And the timber comes down to be replaced by wood.
They have these metaphors – timber and wood – to differentiate
Between states of matter.

I have missed you for many days
In which the world has gone on building,
Tearing down and raising up again under days and nights.
You are the standard by which the visceral world evolves.

The notations of this book
Don't give credit to happenstance.
It's as if we control the many thoughtful ways nothing occurs
By measuring what is and forgetting what is lost.

Your smile, therefore, is meaningless
As is the rest to someone who has seen you only once
Like the sacrifice of trees which is visible to a child only through
Careful observation of his chair, and the author who sees
An obligation to cite origins, but not to those who indifferently
Open the world to his garnered thoughts.

The Jugglers

Bring love to me
        Between the throws
            Oh

Romance of weights
        And objects in
            Threes.

        The bottle flies in
            Articulated
                Space.

The bouncing ball
        The bowling pin
          The dish
          Separate the busy
             Molecules of
                Lips.
        Our spinning hands
          Dispense with air
             Justice
          Mete resistance
             Within arches
                Dives,
Gambling always
        But with precise
          Movements.
          Everything comes
             Like lepers do
                On Christ.

The beginning
        Of something is
The drop
    That remembers
                Each essential
                        Throw.

            Were it not for
                    Matter, we would
                            Miss

What seems an error,
            This scrupulous pitch
                    And catch.

Tattoo

On   the
back of   your lucky
 left shoulder   where you see
  only in reflection   my needle exposes
   an intoxicated man's   2   maculate square inches
    (A pictograph--   The   fulcrum between
     Colossal good   and   evil, not truth
      but luck   in   haphazard
       calligraphy.   After   all does not
        a lucky   man   create
         his   own   truth?)
                              And
                              Do
              you smile or cry when
         for $15 and   30   minutes we
         collaborate: I   who stoically
         transcribe, and   you who provide
         exquisite canvas?   Your black diamond
         eyes shine as they   sample flash from
         the display case   and you smile like
         a Sufi.   "Oh,   what have you
        done?" Nothing   more than employ
        your servant   to express
         desire   and
         illustrate   innocence.

Bow Tie

White gold   cuff link and stud   wearing,
Essentially gazing at they   who are about to wed   we stand like a row of
Waterboys (slaking only apparently a cultural thirst) and overview the relatives, between them representing three
Generations of crying and the lovers' friends, themselves consenting adults, and bemused faces of quite unknowing
Children and the church devotees occupying pews (for perhaps responsibility to traditions of their families, *as is our attendance*).
We submit to the priest reciting rigmarole and see them, bride and groom, each consumed with their solitary being about to
Become the both of them to everyone who thinks of them, and we say to
Ourselves "What is it
Like?" Or in the best man's
Case he recalls the
Saving and spending of thousands of dollars and overtime
Hours working as the plant manager for a paint manufacturer, and the time he saw himself responsible
When she came to him and confessed they were no longer a duo but a triad, and suddenly the world became very
Much a function of its biological invective. He who had once been solitary was now father and husband and proud
And valid are his opinions, and stalwart his reasonings, and grotesque the speed with which time passes, knowing finally the
Richer reality of hope for generations. But now he realizes, the couple standing before the representative of God at this
Moment are quite possibly   only an autonomic   reaction away from
Wetting   themselves

Seminar

"Identify its essence,"
    The poet Robert Bly says holding it aloft.
"Exotic," says one student (a feather in his green cap,
        My name for him is Robin Hood).
           "Foreign," another (this a girl, blonde
                Her sharp nose tiny in profile)
                    "Strange," a third (unseen, his voice appears from
                        Somewhere in the room).

"Wrong," poet Bly exclaims and questions me.
    "It is hollow," I respond.
"Right," says B. His eyes grow sharp.
    Then after the writing assignment
    In which I expound its volcanoes,
        Its empty sockets and how they torment
           (For they twice bewilder me:
                Those dominant
                    Black holes)
    In the hallway, he has taken
        Me aside as the other students pass.

He invites me to Minnesota
    Ostensibly to study poetry.
In turning him down
           I experience
A hollowness
           I'd thought unique to masks.

Narcissus

What is forgiveness?
An acknowledgement that nothing exists as we believed?
Why then hatefully persist
        And require constant patience and other centeredness?
When we do wrong are we not
Halfway to doing right again?
        (The wrong of a wrong demonstrates itself
                On reflection and by the harm done internally,
                        We are thrice invoiced.)
Do we not through others assent to our being?

If we have courage
        To initiate redemption
                And avoid chicanery and the criminal Church
                (God's easier softer way)
                And call resignation faith
        Are we not left only
With ourselves?

I will see you again.
I will smile at you again
Despite everything hurtful we ever did.
Forgiveness is the language of self-love.
        And we are so beautiful
                Our reflections fall in love with us.
                        Without cacophony, cthulhu, chaos
Where is heaven?
        Could I ever be self-aware
                And make you cry?

Fish Logic

You have to use fish logic
    Circle the bowl
        It's all new again.

You work all your life
    Make that bowl as big as possible
        Fish eyes rotating.

All you see is the next room,
    Tell yourself what great imagination
        Pulled Christ up the yardarm.

Only a mind of fish sees enormity.
    A fish mind is a peaceable gallows
        And love an earlobe you pull like a net.

In Anchorage/Modesto they slide over sharks and salmon
    Gaze down into the gazing up.
        God put these scales on your back,

The ocean in your nose and a tail to cut through
    And the bowl reduced in size
        To the ship's deck if need be.

Others cold, but still breathing, breathing.
    We learn of the elements
        Packed against another's silence.

Swim

Pull skull cap and flippers on
Grease up and dive into cold.
The English Channel boils and resists.
And you've a stomach of sea water
      To drive your muscles.

You swim or die it seems.
Ignore the boat monitoring
Exhaustion and the desire to pluck you out,
Water and air alternately kissing
      Your suspended face.

The fish view you as a predator,
Trilled in their language, pass
The word and flee to depths.
They can't bend to your ordered ruling
      Between Neptune and Zeus.

Underwater Sketches

I swim on my hands.
A horseshoe crab underestimates the ocean floor
All he sees are the granules before him
Ignoring the vast expanse of sunken crust.
How much treasure lies buried
And is the ocean itself not treasure?
How clear the music comes to us through the water in our ears.
And how blest are we to know only the song and not its history.
When you bleed into a cup and I drink
Our ritual life is like chumming the ocean:
Who greets us, who sees, recognizes
If we were singular in body but dual in spirit
If we were dual in spirit but singular in body
I ply myself and am abandoned
Mutually to exist.
The many types of animalia
Bead against the shallow skin
The bubble that we see.
But always another layer peeled
Becomes darker and darker
Until at last our eyes are useless
And we see only with our souls
And measure time against our pulses
And deepen into the incomprehensible silence
And extrapolate from nothing the God that still persists
And beach ourselves to that longing, holding fast like a blood-stained anchor
And the sole emblem of our being torn from us to live outside of us
And air and water naked and the sand naked and naked ourselves
And the wash of lightning fixed, universal and perpetual
Death the Maker screams and panting closes
Absolute to be immutably disdained and ever
Forgotten, we who had been anima and
Animus become a scratch on the
Surface of the pearl, black
And consummate as night.
To speak is only to be spoken to.

To listen,
   And if there's knowing it's apart from us.
To quietly proceed
    Fear and bravery feeding each other
And like worms
    Wearing each other's skin
There is a resolution in the souls
    For March and its annual return
Quiet only
     The leaves ache to be borne
The wind to bear
     And you and I
To be.

Daylight

When lack of sleep forces open
The cavern of misering thoughts
And the bell knows its wind and
Echoes from enslavement, and
You and I traverse the blood lines
And make essential martyrs and
Intentional jests out of touching,

When the beast springs to slake
Its lust, and the absolute soul of
Who is knowing encapsulates
Always in the skin of an onion
Busts of the Greeks and torturers
And unintentional beings dragged
From cell memory of their tails,

When the notes fall in paper rains
And ash rains, and the knives held
Distantly to the necks of flowers
Heavy with rain, and the absolute
Blazon imparts its soul to wind and
Steel, you sleep and grow the words
Like a metal sliver in your womb.

And whatever it is we knew emptied
Out. And the storm feathered its
Night with papers. And the tree of
Knowledge dropped fruit on Newton's
Balls and Galileo's head, and again
We saw it torn down what we made
When sleepless eyelids pried apart.

The Lover as Poet
(for sweet JP)

The little girls must be impressed to spread
Their legs, and so he writes with confidence.
What's cast in bronze is the penultimate
Feature, next only to the marble head.

So thus his craft is to consume himself.
Working diligently, perfecting each
Concept and image, he morbidly reach-
Es, then stoops to insert it anally

Into the stanza where it better fits.
He subjects himself to these procedures
Thus to implement what he conjures:
Lines to make the angels bear false witness.

Smiling, concealed in clever anecdotes,
He calls the girls to worship as he gloats.

To a Young Poet with Writer's Block

That thing in you that wants to say will not be long silent.
Young women have a way of reckoning with words
But never forcefully. Language to them is a vehicle demure.

Syllables heating behind your countenance
About to boil are not the tongue of a sword,
But of a hypodermic needle, ready to inject

What murders from within: The singer wants but never gets,
The echo: That which returns to you its call
Is but a voice of nothing, without returning sigh.

So that which angers stays your mouth to cleverness.
You accumulate its power, give time to properly digest,
Then with the care of a lover, place your quiet torments.

And receiving them demurely like one oppressed I
Feel my heart's excessive weight and step to bring its fall.

Grievance

In her infinite wisdom, the dean of students
Has determined the grade of F shall stand.
You admit you struggled with the Epic
Computer program despite having had a
Previous rotation at the same Froedtert
Hospital. You admit you did not prepare
For the rotation and after midterm you
Did not improve your performance enough
To change the preceptor's decision. You have
Failed. You are a failure. You will have to take
The 740 class again and this time if you fail,
You will be kicked out of the school, you worthless
Shit. We hope you learn from this experience.

You ask that I sign, date and return the letter
Informing me of the dean's decision. In
Response I must admit her argument is
Compelling. I have been a shit before, no doubt
Will be a shit again, but during this rotation
I worked well and hard. I made mistakes (I'm
Only human) but did a lot more right than I did
Wrong. I probably deserved a C or even a B
From a generous preceptor, but the asshole
Zimmerman had to fail someone and he chose me.
The dean in her infinite wisdom asked Keiser and
Breslow and possibly you for opinions of the
Grievance, and the answers were no, he's mistaken.
He's a failure. This is heresay. You, Breslow and
Keiser were nowhere near Froedtert Hospital.
You don't know if the shit is me or Zimmerman.

In short, I will not sign, nor date nor return your document.
Though the dean's decision is final that doesn't make it right.
If her intention was to put it all on me, the very least she
Could have done was interview me and allow me to
Defend myself. Therefore I do what she did: Nothing.
And don't waste your time asking me for contributions
After graduation. $12000 in unnecessary tuition
Is $12000 more than you deserve. Thank you and good day.
Please sign and date this document and return it to me.

310

I started out scribbling in a notebook
Then graduated to an old IBM
Selectric. I spent ten hours a day when
The computer lab opened, sometimes on
The same paragraph. I'd watch it grow to
A thousand words, then shrink to twenty, then
I'd eliminate it completely – The
Problem I had with novels, they were too
Big – The mistake I made, I never outlined
Them. – The book kept getting longer, busier,
Convoluted – Out of my control. I
Created more characters and more. I
Fixed them in a house that was more of a
Matrix. They went from room to room, never
Got out. My main character was half man
Half ape and a jazz musician. The Chairman,
His nemesis, wasn't only going
To kill him, but kill and eat him. Never
Finishing the novel, but going on
To start another – About delivering
Pizzas, an autobiography, one
To the CNN van during Jeffrey
Dahmer's trial – He said the hearts tasted
Like steak – He did it he said because
He loved them – Wanting the perfect lover
One without conflict – He injected their
Skulls with hydrochloric acid before
He killed them, then dissolved their bodies in
A barrel of acid in his living
Room. The families of a dozen dead
Sued the city because the cops blew their
Chance to nab him when the fourteen year old
Asian boy wound up naked in the street,
Unable to speak because his brain had
Been poisoned. They called it a lover's spat,
So they left Dahmer and the boy in his

Apartment with human body parts in
The refrigerator. Months later, they
Caught him after several more killings.
Nineteen I think he killed. The families
Settled out of court. The two cops who lost
Their jobs sued the city for lost wages
And won. Dahmer died impaled on a broom
Stick while serving many life sentences
Without chance of parole. I worked for the
Parents of one of the cops, a Polish
Couple: The husband was a complete ass.
I wrote about them too, about the job
And the rain and the old van I used to
Haul the broken concrete to the landfill.
And the job and the many stories of
The job. And later turning to poems.
Changing my career, but still having to
Write, and publications coming faster
Until finally the book was finished
And so was I until I turned to drugs.

Poetry Notes

A Painting
   The tree speaking is a reference to Dante's *Inferno*, specifically Canto XIII, depicting the 7th Circle, Ring 2 in which the souls of suicides are physically confined to trees. The soul of a dead man speaks to Dante and Virgil upon having a branch painfully broken.

Jugglers
   Much of this poem was inspired by Heidegger (German philosopher, Martin Heidegger 1889-1976), as in the "Whatness of a Thing".

Narcissus
   The phrase "God's easier softer way" is derived from the "AA Big Book" (*Alcoholics Anonymous-The Big Book,* currently in its fourth edition; published by Alcoholics Anonymous World Services, Inc.; February 10, 2002).
   Cthulhu is the name of a character created by science fiction / psychological exploration writer, H. P. Lovecraft. It first appeared in the short story "The Call of Cthulhu", published in the magazine *Weird Tales* in 1928. Cthulhu is part octopus, dragon, and human, with tentacles on its head and having a scaly body, with rudimentary wings. Imprisoned, but expected to make a return, Cthulhu is a persistent character in Lovecraft's writing. Cthulhu is a subconscious source of anxiety for mankind, and is worshiped by a number of evil cults.

Fish Logic
   This poem was written by Mark while he was in a mental hospital.
   A yardarm is either end of a yard for a square rigged sail on a ship, the yard being a long horizontal spar (pole) on a mast from which sails are set.

Swim
   This poem, in some of its aspects, pays homage to American poet Hilda Doolittle (1886-1961).

CPSIA information can be obtained at www.ICGtesting.com
Printed in the USA
LVOW091309030712

288699LV00001B/5/P